Depression is NOT Your Destiny

A Practical & Proven Step-by-Step Guide on How to Experience a Life of Emotional Freedom, NOW!

Brett Coleman

To my son, Cash...

You are my greatest inspiration, my light in the darkest moments, and the reason I refused to let depression win. Every step I took toward healing, every battle I fought, and every breakthrough I achieved was fueled by the love I have for you. You reminded me that life is worth fighting for, that joy is still possible, and that you are my purpose—far greater than my pain.

This book exists because of you. Because when I looked at you, I knew I had to find a way out—not just for myself, but for the father you deserve to have. You gave me the strength to believe in something better, to rebuild, and to prove that **Depression is NOT Destiny!**

Thank you for being my reason, my motivation, and my greatest gift.

I love you endlessly,

Dad

Contents

How to Use This Playbook

This is Your Blueprint

THIS IS YOUR BLUEPRINT to reclaiming emotional freedom, taking back your mind and building resilience from depression and anxiety. Each chapter offers actionable insights, practical exercises for action and transformative lessons to guide you in your journey of creating positive mental health habits that reshape your paradigm.

This is an easy yet profound step by step playbook that provides you with the *"how's* and *why's"* so you'll have a clear understanding of the ideas being offered.

You will be provided thorough explanations of *how* it works (mechanics) and *why* it works (the science or logic behind it). This understanding builds trust in the process of transformation.

My intention is to equip you with a clear, powerful, and transformative action plan designed to spark real, lasting change in your life. As someone who has emerged from the depths of debilitating depression, paralyzing anxiety, and relentless suicidal ideation—and now lives medication-free—I intimately understand the crushing weight of feeling lost, broken, and uncertain about where to even begin the healing process.

I Know How Hard it is for You

I wrote this guide because I know how overwhelming it can be to face a mountain of advice or a long, complex book when you're struggling just to get through the day. Instead, I've condensed years of hard-earned wisdom and actionable strategies into a simple, step-by-step framework that is both manageable and effective.

This book isn't just a collection of ideas; it's a lifeline. It's designed to empower you with the tools and clarity to take immediate steps toward healing and emotional freedom—without adding to the overwhelm you may already feel. My hope is that each step will bring you closer to rediscovering your strength, rebuilding your confidence, and reclaiming the life you deserve.

This isn't just about creating change; it's about giving you the courage and clarity to take that crucial first step. Because I've been where you are, and I can tell you this: healing is possible, and it begins right here!

I've Been There

For years, I battled **debilitating depression, paralyzing anxiety, PTSD, chronic insomnia, and major suicidal ideation**—all while being over-prescribed more than **twenty different medications**, eventually diagnosed with **treatment-resistant depression**. I nearly lost my life and walked away from a six-figure career, feeling there was no way out. But I refused to accept that as my reality. Today, I am **cured from all of it and medication-free, and thriving.**

Through this book, a website and various social media platforms, it's my mission to give you the **tools, knowledge, belief, and courage** to transform your life. I want to help you become **more confident, more effective, and more fulfilled** by discovering the **best version of your-self**— you deserve to live a life that is **bold, limitless, and free.**

I am building a powerful community of warriors—people who refused to let depression, anxiety, or any mental health struggle define them. Together, we will break the stigma, rewrite the narrative, and show the world what true strength looks like.

Your breakthrough starts now.

Let's take this journey together, and let's prove that no matter how dark it gets, there is always a way forward.

Depression is NOT Your Destiny

T HIS PROVEN SYSTEM EXPLAINS how to overcome anxiety and depression and explains why these methods work. By combining action with understanding, you'll not only feel empowered to change but you will also gain clarity about the mechanisms behind your transformation.

By the time you finish this book you will have the knowledge and tools to:

- Recognize core principles for success

- Apply Practical Exercises to improve your well-being

- Know the How and Why of each action step

- Apply Small, Consistent Steps of Action for progression

- Stay Committed to the Process

- Curious for Continued Growth

Commit to the journey, trust the process, and watch yourself grow into the person you were born to be.

"Dream your life, live your dream!"

—Brett Coleman, Author

Chapter One

You Are Not Your Depression

SIX KEY LESSONS:

1. Depression is a State of Mind, not Your Identity or Your Destiny

It is not who you are , but rather what you're going through. Recognize this separation, create a space to begin to take action so you can redefine life on your terms. Understanding this truth is the first step toward reclaiming your life.

2. Your Thoughts are not Absolute Truths

Depression often feeds on negative thoughts and distorted thinking, which leads to a distorted reality. Learning to recognize, question and reframe these thoughts can begin to release you from the grips of depression. Start to replace false beliefs with empowering truths.

3. Your Brain can be Rewired

Neuroplasticity allows you to change patterns of thinking and behavior. Through mindfulness and intentional practice, you can create new, positive mental habits. Changing your perception is essential and requires a deliberate intention to challenge and replace old patterns with new empowering ones that align with the new life you are creating.

4. Your Subconscious Mind can be Reprogrammed

The subconscious mind is like fertile soil, it grows whatever seeds you plant, whether positive or negative. Through techniques like affirmations, visualization, and consistent mental conditioning, you can reprogram your subconscious to support a new, healthier narrative. Repetition and emotional engagement are the keys to embedding new beliefs.

5. Your Perception Shapes Your Experience...Your Story Creates Your Circumstances

Your life is not set in stone. By shifting your perspective, you can begin to see possibilities rather than limitations. Altering how you perceive yourself and your situation transforms your reality. Visualize the new "you," and feel what it's like living that new reality. As you align your thoughts, feelings and actions with this new story, your reality will begin to reflect the changes.

6. You Have the Power to Change

Even in your darkest moments, the potential for change exists within you. Focus on daily habits that support positive and healthy habits such as journaling, practicing gratitude and mediating. Small, consistent actions can lead to profound transformations and major mental breakthroughs over time.

EXERCISE: How to Challenge Negative Thoughts

How it Works:

Identifying and labeling any negative thought externalizes it, making it easier to evaluate. Writing it down also prevents it from endlessly repeating itself in your mind.

Why it Works:

Depressive thoughts often feel automatic and overwhelming. By identifying them, you are taking a significant step toward separating yourself from the thoughts and regaining a sense of self-control.

SIX ACTION STEPS:

#1. Thought Reframing

Write down the recurring negative thoughts (e.g., "I'm a failure," "I feel hopeless")

Replace the old paradigm by reframing the thoughts with more positive and accurate statements (e.g., I am learning and growing from this challenge that I am facing). Repeat this process by writing it down and by saying it aloud, even recording it into your phone. By doing so you will begin to weaken and eventually destroy the power of any negative thoughts.

#2. Paradigm Awareness Chart

Draw two columns. In the first, list any recurring limiting beliefs tied to depression (e.g. *I'm not good enough* or *My life will never get better*).

In the second column, write empowering alternatives (e.g. "*I am a miracle in God's highest form of creation and I am getting better every day!*" Or "*My efforts create change*"). Review and affirm these empowering beliefs daily to reshape your perspective and reinforce a new paradigm.

#3. Reprogram Your Subconscious

Create 3-5 affirmations that reflect your desired mindset (e.g., "*I am strong, resilient, and worthy of joy*"). Spend 10-15 minutes each morning and evening repeating these affirmations while visualizing your future self in the present moment. Pair an emotion to deepen the feeling.

#4. Rewrite Your Story

Write a detailed narrative of the perception you have of your current life story. Focus on areas where depression has the biggest impact on you. Now write a new story of the image you have of your new self, including resiliency, success, emotional balance and fulfillment. Read this story aloud daily and make improvements that align with the new vision you have of your new life.

#5. Build Momentum Through Small Wins

At the end of each day before going to bed, write down three-five things you are grateful for and one small action or idea you will take tomorrow to support your mental health goals. This will reinforce positive momentum and help you focus on progress even in the smallest of form.

#6. Challenge Negative Thoughts

Ask yourself:

- "What evidence supports this thought?"
- "What evidence contradicts it?"

Examine both sides.

- Supporting evidence: *"I've felt unhappy for months."*
- Contradicting evidence: *"Even through my challenges, I am experiencing happy moments."*

Depression often distorts reality, exaggerating the negatives and often ignoring the positives. Challenging the thoughts with evidence brings this truth to the surface and breaks the cycle of catastrophizing, helping to balance your perspective.

Daily Reflections (Repeat Daily for the Week)

Write or reflect on these questions each day to strengthen your awareness and shift your mindset in real time.

1. Today I became aware of a thought that didn't serve me. That thought was:

   → Replace it with a more empowering thought:

2. I visualized my future self feeling _____.

   → What did that version of me believe about life, healing, and myself?

3. A small moment of emotional victory I experienced today:

   → (Even a breath, a smile, or a pause counts.)

4. Today I chose to show myself love by:

   → (Action, mindset, or self-care choice.)

5. One word that describes how I want to feel tomorrow:

Weekly Reflection (Complete at the End of the Week)

Use these questions to process the week's progress and recommit to your healing.

1. What limiting belief or emotion did I begin to break free from this week?

2. When did I feel most aligned with the version of me I'm becoming?

3. What inner resistance showed up? How did I respond to it?

4. What insights or wins did I experience this week, no matter how small?

5. What is one powerful intention I'm carrying into next week?

    → My intention:

Optional Weekly Practice

Visualization Activation: Spend 5–10 minutes in meditation or quiet reflection. Imagine your healed, whole, future self. What do you see, feel, and believe? Journal about it.

Anchor Phrase: Choose a simple mantra to repeat each morning this week.

→ Example: "I am free. I am healing. I am enough."

→ Your phrase:

_____

Chapter Two

Set Your Intention

SIX KEY LESSONS:

1. Clarity is Power

Overcoming depression requires a clear vision of what you want to achieve. Setting a specific intention, such as "I am becoming more hopeful each day" or "I am reconnecting with joy," gives your mind a target to work toward. Without clarity or a new narrative, it's easy to remain stuck in a state of uncertainty, which can lead to feelings of hopelessness.

2. Intentions Guide Your Focus

Depression often thrives on negativity and overwhelm. By setting an intention, you are training your mind to focus on possibilities instead of problems. For example, focusing on building small daily habits for well-being and emotional balance, shifts your attention from feeling powerless to having control over your thoughts.

3. Intentions are Anchored in the Present

Unlike goals, which are often future-oriented, intentions center you in the present moment. For instance, setting an intention like "I will practice self-compassion today" empowers you to make immediate, positive changes regardless of circumstances.

4. The Subconscious Mind Responds to Intention

Intentions act as instructions for your subconscious mind. When repeated consistently with an elevated emotion, they align your thoughts, feelings and actions to your desired state. This creates a ripple effect that strengthens positive behaviors and weakens depressive patterns.

5. Small Intentions Build Momentum

Overcoming depression doesn't happen overnight, just as you didn't become depressed overnight. But setting small achievable intentions compound over time. Having an arsenal of powerful intentions fosters consistency and will build a sense of accomplishment within you.

How to: Set a Daily Connection Intention
Focus on one small way to connect with someone else each day and express 1-2 things you are grateful for. Remember, you are rewiring your brain for success, so this interaction is not intended for you to dwell on how bad things are, but rather on the small things you are expressing gratitude for.

6. Intentions Create Emotional Shifts

Depression often suppresses hope and positivity. Your intention to look for something good in your day and acknowledging that as an accomplishment creates confidence. It also retrains your brain to experience uplifting emotions, which counteract depressive states.

EXERCISE: How to Create a Gratitude and Positivity Check-In

How it Works:

This will redirect focus to the positive and begin to redirect you from the negative by engaging neural pathways for optimism.

Why it Works:

Counters negative bias and boosts emotional resilience. It also enhances mind-body connection by lowering stress hormones such as cortisol while increasing the feel-good hormones serotonin and dopamine.

SIX ACTION STEPS:

#1. Create a New You

At the end of each day, visualize yourself as the new you, while at the same time giving thanks for all of your super blessings of that day. Then add a feeling to this visualization that evokes an emotion of gratitude. Hold the feeling of that image as you fall off to sleep so that it impresses a new image on the screen of your subconscious mind throughout your various stages of sleep.

#2. Set Daily Intentions

At the beginning of each morning set a clear intention for that day. Example: "Today I will focus on staying present in each moment of the day."

"I will manage negative thoughts, feelings or emotions by recognizing they are not my reality."

#3. Have a Clear Vision

Set your intention with clarity by defining a clear vision of what you want and expect! Then release the "how" by trusting your intention will unfold organically, without you knowing exactly how.

Example: "I don't need to control every detail. I trust my intention will guide and provide me with the right opportunities, actions and outcomes."

#4. Anchor Present Moment Intentions

Practice mindful breathing for 5-10 minutes while repeating a present focused intention such as, "I choose peace in this moment" or "I am perfectly balanced in this moment." You can use this exercise anytime you begin to feel yourself becoming overwhelmed or disconnected.

#5. The Power of Detachment

Sit in meditation seeing yourself as who you would be without the feelings of anxiety or depression. Then set the intention by repeating the affirmation I am detached from negative thoughts, feelings or emotions.

#6. Reflect and Savor

Take a deep breath and as you exhale, pin a feeling of gratitude on the top five things you are grateful for. It is very important you induce an intense feeling to this exercise so that it signals the brain to focus on the good aspects of life. In doing so, you will eventually notice a shift in how you begin to counteract the negative emotions all too common with anxiety and depression.

Daily Reflections (Repeat Daily for the Week)

Write or reflect on these questions each day to strengthen your awareness and shift your mindset in real time.

1. Today I became aware of a thought that didn't serve me. That thought was:

   → Replace it with a more empowering thought:

2. I visualized my future self feeling _____.

   → What did that version of me believe about life, healing, and myself?

3. A small moment of emotional victory I experienced today:

   → (Even a breath, a smile, or a pause counts.)

4. Today I chose to show myself love by:

   → (Action, mindset, or self-care choice.)

5. One word that describes how I want to feel tomorrow:

Weekly Reflection (Complete at the End of the Week)

Use these questions to process the week's progress and recommit to your healing.

1. What limiting belief or emotion did I begin to break free from this week?

2. When did I feel most aligned with the version of me I'm becoming?

3. What inner resistance showed up? How did I respond to it?

4. What insights or wins did I experience this week, no matter how small?

5. What is one powerful intention I'm carrying into next week?

   → My intention:

Optional Weekly Practice

Visualization Activation: Spend 5–10 minutes in meditation or quiet reflection. Imagine your healed, whole, future self. What do you see, feel, and believe? Journal about it.

Anchor Phrase: Choose a simple mantra to repeat each morning this week.

→ Example: "I am free. I am healing. I am enough."

→ Your phrase:

_____

Chapter Three

Self Awareness: The Foundation for Overcoming Depression and Anxiety

SIX KEY LESSONS

1. Understanding Resistance

Recognize whenever humans initiate change, we are inevitably going to be met with resistance. Having this understanding can greatly contribute to our success in overcoming our state of mental health. The resistance often comes in the form of limiting beliefs that have been programmed into our subconscious mind, which creates a false perception of reality. These limiting ideas need to be closely examined and understood as habits of the mind, and do not determine your fate.

2. Pay Attention to Your Inner Dialogue

Your self talk greatly influences your emotions and behaviors. Becoming aware of your inner dialogue allows you to challenge and replace it with more supportive and constructive narratives.

3. Identify Your Emotional Patterns

Depression and anxiety often come with recurring emotional states, such as fear, guilt or hopelessness. Being aware of these patterns enables you to address them before they spiral out of control.

4. Recognize the Mind-Body Connection

Your mental state affects your physical well-being and vice versa. Self-awareness includes noticing how physical sensations, like tension and/or fatigue, signal underlying emotional struggles so we can begin taking steps to address them.

5. Distinguish Between Facts and Fears

Anxiety often stems from imagined scenarios or worst-case thinking, while depression can magnify feelings of inadequacy. Becoming aware of when you're mistaking fear for facts can greatly reduce mental distress.

6. Be Honest About Your Needs and Boundaries

Self-awareness includes understanding what you need to feel safe, supported, and balanced. It also means recognizing when to say "no" or when to ask for help without guilt or shame.

EXERCISE: How to Have a Mind-Body Connection

How it Works:

The mind-body connection refers to the dynamic relationship between your thoughts, emotions, and physical health. This connection is mediated by a complex interaction of biological, neurological, and psychological processes. Your brain sends signals to the body through the nervous system, influencing physical functions such as heart rate, digestion, and muscle tension.

Why it Works:

Our mental and physical systems are deeply integrated. They continuously interact and influence each other, ensuring survival, regulating emotions, and maintaining overall health.

SIX ACTION STEPS:

#1. Track Your Tension

Spend 5-10 minutes lying down or sitting comfortably. Close your eyes and mentally scan your entire body. Notice any messages of limiting beliefs that include, fear, doubt, worry, and worse-case scenarios. Then recognize any areas of your body that may be affected by the negative energy of these thoughts.

Ask yourself:

- What might this physical sensation be telling me about my emotional state?
- How can I reframe the thoughts creating this state of being?

#2. Practice Thought Awareness

Keep a journal noting situations, thoughts or interactions that arise in an attempt to keep you stuck in a state of anxiety or depression.

Write down any limiting beliefs...

Your Immediate thoughts and feelings towards them...

How you responded (e.g., avoided, overreacted, withdrew.)

At the end of each week, review your journaling to help you identify habit patterns. This clarity allows you to develop strategies to overcome any negative effects of your limiting beliefs.

#3. Challenge Your Fears

Ask the following questions:

- Are these thoughts based on fact or fears?
- How will I reframe those thoughts into more positive or neutral beliefs?

Example:

Change *"My life is hopeless"* or *"Something bad is going to happen"* to

"This is happening for me, not to me", or *"This is for my betterment, not my detriment"*, or *"I am better because of it!"*

#4. Clarify Your Needs and Boundaries

Divide a sheet of paper into two columns.

Column 1: Write down your core needs for emotional and physical well-being (e.g., rest, alone time, connection, support, and reassurance).

Column 2: Write down boundaries you can set to protect these needs (e.g., "*I will limit my conversations with negative people.*" "*I will make time for myself without feeling guilty about it.*")

Review this list regularly and practice reinforcing your boundaries in small, manageable ways.

#5. Conscious Detachment

Observe your thoughts as if you were a lifeguard at the beach watching the waves roll in from a lifeguard tower. Rather than getting caught up in the undertow of the waves, you simply watch & observe them. Same with your thoughts, just watch them and you will quickly realize, you are separate from the negative thoughts.

You can add another element to this exercise either by visualizing or by writing;

- What do you know to be true, based on evidence?

- What are you imaging or assuming might happen, even if it's unlikely or unproven?

- What evidence do I have that this fear will come true?

- What's the evidence against it?

- What's a more realistic or balanced perspective?

Using the lifeguard example, observe your thought process and if you feel it would be helpful, write out the preceding questions with answers.

You will be amazed at how well this begins to diminish the feelings of fear.

#6. 4-4-6-2 Mind-Body Reset

This quick exercise is designed to reduce stress and reconnect your mind and body in just a few minutes, perfect for the workplace.

- Breathe in for 4 seconds
- Hold for 4 seconds
- Release for 6 seconds, and
- Hold for 2 seconds

Repeat 3-5 times for a quick reset and relaxation.

Daily Reflections (Repeat Daily for the Week)

Write or reflect on these questions each day to strengthen your awareness and shift your mindset in real time.

1. Today I became aware of a thought that didn't serve me. That thought was:

    → Replace it with a more empowering thought:

2. I visualized my future self feeling _____.

    → What did that version of me believe about life, healing, and myself?

3. A small moment of emotional victory I experienced today:

    → (Even a breath, a smile, or a pause counts.)

4. Today I chose to show myself love by:

    → (Action, mindset, or self-care choice.)

5. One word that describes how I want to feel tomorrow:

Weekly Reflection (Complete at the End of the Week)

Use these questions to process the week's progress and recommit to your healing.

1. What limiting belief or emotion did I begin to break free from this week?

2. When did I feel most aligned with the version of me I'm becoming?

3. What inner resistance showed up? How did I respond to it?

4. What insights or wins did I experience this week, no matter how small?

5. What is one powerful intention I'm carrying into next week?

   → My intention:

Optional Weekly Practice

Visualization Activation: Spend 5–10 minutes in meditation or quiet reflection. Imagine your healed, whole, future self. What do you see, feel, and believe? Journal about it.

Anchor Phrase: Choose a simple mantra to repeat each morning this week.

→ Example: "I am free. I am healing. I am enough."

→ Your phrase:

_____

Chapter Four

Self Knowledge: Your Perception Shapes Your Reality

SIX KEY LESSONS

1. Self-Knowledge is a Cornerstone of Personal Growth

Through self-knowledge you have the power to take the pain out of any fearful moment in your life by understanding what matters most in any unwanted moment of life is your perception of the situation, and not what you fearfully imagining is happening to you in that moment.

Learning you have the power to dissolve fear from any moment in life is by having the knowledge that perception creates the reality, rather than the actual event.

2. Self-Knowledge Increases Emotional Intelligence

By understanding how your emotions trigger reactions, you gain greater control of how you can choose to respond rather than react. Recognizing response patterns allows you to adjust to situations and challenges more effectively.

3. Self-Knowledge Empowers Decision-Making

Having a clear understanding of how old paradigms can be holding you back, allows you to be open to areas of your mind you want to reshape and areas of your life you want to improve.

4. Self-Knowledge Fosters Resilience and Self-Acceptance

Recognizing any areas of self-limitation that are tied to past experiences can help you change your inner narrative providing you with greater self-compassion and strength. Journaling, therapy, and introspection helps you reframe past experiences and promote a growth mindset.

5. Rediscovering Your Purpose

Clarifying your core values, passions, goals and reflecting on what truly matters to you, can rekindle a sense of purpose, even in small ways. Depression often thrives on feelings of aimlessness or disconnection. Aligning with your purpose fosters hope and motivation, which can counteract feelings associated with depression.

6. Empowering Change Through Insight

Self-Knowledge equips you with the insight needed to create actionable change. Realizing any form of negativity, like isolation can intensify feelings of hopelessness. Consider getting involved with social activities to create momentum toward healing.

Self-knowledge is not a magic cure, but it certainly lays out the groundwork for meaningful change by helping you understand and address the unique factors contributing to your depression. Paired with strategies like mindfulness, and supportive habits, self-knowledge can guide you from understanding your struggles to overcoming them.

Exercise: How to Pause and Identify the Fear

How it Works:

When fear arises, pause and describe what you're thinking and how you're feeling.

Why it Works:

This simple yet powerful exercise interrupts the automatic stress or fear response by shifting activity from the amygdala to the prefrontal cortex. When you pause, you're better able to analyze the situation more objectively instead of overreacting emotionally.

SIX ACTION STEPS:

#1. Take a Deep Breath and Name Whatever Feeling You are Experiencing

Pay close attention to all of your emotions and identify each of them.

#2. Write Down and/or Closely Examine the Exact Thoughts Running Through Your Mind

Doing so, you will begin to recognize a habit pattern of how your thoughts are creating the feelings and how the feelings are creating your reality, remembering negative thoughts are based on a false or imagined premise.

#3. Ask, "What am I imagining is happening right now?"

#4. Then ask, "What is actually happening right now?"

#5. Compare Your Imagined Reality to the Actual Reality

Do a thorough examination of what you're thinking and how you're feeling is predominately only taking place in your imagination.

#6. Validate Your Experience

Once you've identified the fear and affirmed your feelings are based on false pretenses, you will have taken one step closer to building your emotional resilience.

Daily Reflections (Repeat Daily for the Week)

Write or reflect on these questions each day to strengthen your aware-ness and shift your mindset in real time.

1. Today I became aware of a thought that didn't serve me. That thought was:

    → Replace it with a more empowering thought:

2. I visualized my future self feeling _____.

    → What did that version of me believe about life, healing, and myself?

3. A small moment of emotional victory I experienced today:

    → (Even a breath, a smile, or a pause counts.)

4. Today I chose to show myself love by:

    → (Action, mindset, or self-care choice.)

5. One word that describes how I want to feel tomorrow:

Weekly Reflection (Complete at the End of the Week)

Use these questions to process the week's progress and recommit to your healing.

1. What limiting belief or emotion did I begin to break free from this week?

2. When did I feel most aligned with the version of me I'm becoming?

3. What inner resistance showed up? How did I respond to it?

4. What insights or wins did I experience this week, no matter how small?

5. What is one powerful intention I'm carrying into next week?

   → My intention:

Optional Weekly Practice

Visualization Activation: Spend 5–10 minutes in meditation or quiet reflection. Imagine your healed, whole, future self. What do you see, feel, and believe? Journal about it.

Anchor Phrase: Choose a simple mantra to repeat each morning this week.

→ Example: "I am free. I am healing. I am enough."

→ Your phrase:

_____

Chapter Five

Debunking a Fearful Imagination

SIX KEY LESSONS:

1. F.E.A.R. — False Evidence Appearing Real

Fearful thoughts are often projections of "what might happen" rather than reflections of what is actually happening. Recognizing this distinction allows you to respond calmly to the moment rather than reacting to imagined threats.

2. Fearful Thoughts Are Hypotheses, Not Facts

Fearful imagination can intensify depression by creating worst-case scenarios and distorting reality. By learning to challenge and debunk these imagined fears, you can alleviate depressive symptoms and foster emotional resilience.

3. Separate What You Know from What You Imagine

Fearful thoughts are often assumptions your mind generates, not absolute truths. When you treat your fears as hypotheses, you can question their validity instead of accepting them as reality. This will greatly reduce the emotional weight of fearful thoughts, creating a space for you to view them as not being inevitable outcomes.

4. Fact vs. Fiction

Fear thrives on uncertainty by blending facts with imagined outcomes. Distinguishing between the two helps you see the situation more clearly. Once you expose the truth about your imagined fears, you quickly begin to realize most of your fears are only speculative, allowing you to focus on actionable realities rather than imagined fears.

5. Challenge the Worst-Case Scenario

Fearful imagination often focuses on the worst possible outcome, I know first-hand the debilitating effects this type of mindset can have on a person. Ruminating on the "worst case what-ifs'" is what I named it. This destructive type of thinking nearly ended my life because of how intense and out of control my thoughts became.

Facing the worst-case scenarios head-on greatly diminishes the power it has and strengthens your ability to overcome challenges. Remember, the greatest challenge lies within your mind, once you understand this, everything changes!

6. Replace Fearful Thoughts with Constructive Questions

Fearful thoughts are repetitive and extremely unproductive. Shifting your attention and beginning to ask yourself constructive questions, greatly reframes your mindset. Constructive questioning focuses your energy on solutions, reducing rumination and placing you back in control of your thoughts, and ultimately your life!

EXERCISE: How to Reframe the Fearful Story

How it Works:

Challenging your story about the imagined situation or event, puts situations in perspective, and removes you from the downward cycle of hopeless thoughts, feelings, and emotions.

Why it Works:

Reframing a fearful story works to cure depression by addressing its root cause: distorted perceptions and negative thought patterns.

SIX ACTION STEPS:

#1. Write Down the Fearful Story

#2. Identify the Facts Versus Your Perceived Fears About Them

#3. Rewrite the Story From a Balanced Perspective

Ask yourself, "Who would I be and how would I feel RIGHT NOW without my attachment to this imagined fear?"

#4. Shift Your Narratives

When you create a shift in your narratives, you will reduce the emotional pain, regain a sense of control and create a healthy mental environment for healing and growth.

#5. Rewire Your Brain

By creating a new habit to consistently reframe imagined fears, you are also creating new neural pathways that support a healthy way of thinking. This will signal the brain as your "new norm," and eventually becomes your default mode. Meditation and visualization by far had the biggest impact on me. It literally took my mind from a suicidal state to supernatural state!

#6. Strengthen Optimism and Build Resilience

When you focus on the infinite possibilities for your life, rather than your past failures or shortcomings, you're creating a shift that cultivates optimism, which is crucial for countering feelings of hopelessness that fuel depression and anxiety.

Daily Reflections (Repeat Daily for the Week)

Write or reflect on these questions each day to strengthen your awareness and shift your mindset in real time.

1. Today I became aware of a thought that didn't serve me. That thought was:

   → Replace it with a more empowering thought:

2. I visualized my future self feeling _____.

   → What did that version of me believe about life, healing, and myself?

3. A small moment of emotional victory I experienced today:

   → (Even a breath, a smile, or a pause counts.)

4. Today I chose to show myself love by:

   → (Action, mindset, or self-care choice.)

5. One word that describes how I want to feel tomorrow:

Weekly Reflection (Complete at the End of the Week)

Use these questions to process the week's progress and recommit to your healing.

1. What limiting belief or emotion did I begin to break free from this week?

2. When did I feel most aligned with the version of me I'm becoming?

3. What inner resistance showed up? How did I respond to it?

4. What insights or wins did I experience this week, no matter how small?

5. What is one powerful intention I'm carrying into next week?

   → My intention:

Optional Weekly Practice

Visualization Activation: Spend 5–10 minutes in meditation or quiet reflection. Imagine your healed, whole, future self. What do you see, feel, and believe? Journal about it.

Anchor Phrase: Choose a simple mantra to repeat each morning this week.

→ Example: "I am free. I am healing. I am enough."

→ Your phrase:

_____

Chapter Six

Focus on What You Can Control

SIX KEY LESSONS:

1. Restore a Sense of Control

Direct your energy, attention, and actions toward aspects of situations within your control rather than worrying about things beyond your reach. I also encourage you to practice acceptance in certain situations where you have no control. This mindset helps you take proactive steps to improve your circumstances while also letting go of unnecessary stress over uncontrollable factors.

2. Take Responsibility for Your Actions

Accept accountability for your behavior and choices without blaming others for external factors. This will inevitably help you realize you have the power to regain control over your choices and your life.

3. The Power of Letting Go

Focus on what you can control, by doing so you shift from a victim mindset to an empowered one. You will also notice this helps you stay grounded, even in challenging situations, because you have placed your attention on an intention to take actionable steps, this will undoubtedly begin to diminish feelings of helplessness.

4. Building Resilience and Empowerment

Focusing on what you can control, requires acknowledging the things you cannot change and then consciously releasing your attachment to them. This doesn't mean ignoring problems or pretending they don't exist, rather accepting that some outcomes are beyond your influence, decreasing and even eliminating unnecessary worry.

5. Identify What You Can Control

You have control over your thoughts, emotions, and reactions. The choices you make and the actions you take are within your control. It's important to recognize you have control over your interaction and communication with others, and the ability to set boundaries as necessary, this is all part of regaining control.

6. What You Cannot Control

You have no control over other people's actions, opinions, or feelings. There's nothing within your power that can control the outcomes of unexpected events or external circumstances. The past or future is definitely something out of one's control. Focusing on what you can control means deliberately choosing to prioritize areas where your efforts can be better suited to create positive change.

EXERCISE: How to Regain Your Power

How it Works:

The following action steps will help you minimize the mental strain caused by worrying about uncontrollable factors.

Why it Works:

This exercise is extremely effective in reducing the feelings of hopelessness and empowers you to take constructive action. It redirects your energy towards actions that will lead to tangible results.

SIX ACTION STEPS:

#1. Observe & Ask

Observe.

- Recognize everything in your control (e.g., your attitude, your perception and all of the choices you have available to you.

Ask.

- Is there any evidence for fear-based thoughts?

- Is there evidence against them?

- What is a more balanced perspective I can adopt right now in this moment that will improve my outcomes?

#2. Write

Write down everything that feels overwhelming or fearful about the moment and follow up by writing out the answer to the previous questions. Writing it out expedites the process of being able to quickly identify how inaccurate your perspective may be. The whole idea is to create a shift in the way you're perceiving situations, and how your perception creates your reality.

#3. Commit to Small Achievable Goals

Take one small yet positive and effective action step towards.

- Take a long walk

- Prepare an enjoyable meal

- Journaling for 10 minutes on your new life is incredibly healthy and effective.

    Rather than journaling to "feel better," commit to writing out short stories about your new life that reframe your thoughts and reshape your paradigm.

Accomplishing small goals places your focus on obtaining manageable goals.

#4. Walking Meditation

As you walk, focus on an object off in the distance, while at the same time observe your breathing. This will activate your parasympathetic nervous system, reducing the physical symptoms of anxiety and providing a sense of control over your emotional state. The combination of redirecting your focus, on a specific object while being mindful of your breathing, is an excellent hack for turning off the feelings of anxiety.

#5. Create a "Calming Down" Routine for Triggering Moments

Breath work, soothing instrumental music and stretching is a very effective way to calm your mind & body. Regaining control over your emotional state teaches your brain that you can manage the anxiety instead of it spiraling you out of control.

#6. Practice Gratitude

Gratitude has been described as the healthiest of all human emotions. I understand first-hand how difficult it can be to feel good about anything when you're feeling extremely bad about everything. That is why I am encouraging you to start with baby steps for this practice and watch how quickly the momentum picks up as you make gratitude part of your daily practice.

Examples:

- "I will commit to a 10-minute walk today."

- "I will make time to meditate this morning."

- "I didn't overreact or ruminate over something that caused me to feel anxious."

These small steps will lead to big wins when they are part of your daily practice.

That's why I strongly encourage you to commit to making these action steps part of your daily routine. Reframing your thoughts, setting achievable goals, and practicing controlled breathing along with meditation, you redirect your energy toward constructive actions that support healing.

These steps provide tangible ways to quickly regain control over your life and create a solid foundation for overcoming anxiety and depression.

By implementing a calming down routine and daily gratitude practice, you redirect your focus to achievable, controllable actions that foster a sense of stability and growth.

These tools reinforce your ability to manage emotions and gradually replace anxiety and depression with feelings of self-control and personal power.

Daily Reflections (Repeat Daily for the Week)

Write or reflect on these questions each day to strengthen your awareness and shift your mindset in real time.

1. Today I became aware of a thought that didn't serve me. That thought was:

   → Replace it with a more empowering thought:

2. I visualized my future self feeling _____.

   → What did that version of me believe about life, healing, and myself?

3. A small moment of emotional victory I experienced today:

   → (Even a breath, a smile, or a pause counts.)

4. Today I chose to show myself love by:

   → (Action, mindset, or self-care choice.)

5. One word that describes how I want to feel tomorrow:

Weekly Reflection (Complete at the End of the Week)

Use these questions to process the week's progress and recommit to your healing.

1. What limiting belief or emotion did I begin to break free from this week?

2. When did I feel most aligned with the version of me I'm becoming?

3. What inner resistance showed up? How did I respond to it?

4. What insights or wins did I experience this week, no matter how small?

5. What is one powerful intention I'm carrying into next week?

   → My intention:

Optional Weekly Practice

Visualization Activation: Spend 5–10 minutes in meditation or quiet reflection. Imagine your healed, whole, future self. What do you see, feel, and believe? Journal about it.

Anchor Phrase: Choose a simple mantra to repeat each morning this week.

→ Example: "I am free. I am healing. I am enough."

→ Your phrase:

_____

Chapter Seven

Faith: Having a Belief in What You Cannot Yet See

SIX KEY LESSONS:

1. Trust in Possibilities

In any moment, you can cultivate a belief in unseen possibilities, which is essential for overcoming anxiety and depression. Choose to focus on what's possible instead of what feels overwhelming or uncertain. This shift in your focus reduces the power of fear and strengthens your belief in Faith.

2. Trust the Process of Healing

Belief in what you cannot see is about trusting in possibilities, progress and outcomes that aren't immediately visible. It involves faith in your own capacity to grow, heal, and transform, even when the evidence isn't apparent. Trust that the small, consistent steps you take daily contribute to your long-term healing. By committing to daily actions, like the ones being offered to you in this step by step playbook, will help you build momentum and give you the results you want.

Trusting in the process will be vital to your success and reduces any pressure to "fix everything now," which alleviates anxiety and promotes patience and hope.

Once I was able to calm my mind and practice patience, my out of control thoughts, feelings, and emotions gradually became easier to manage, control and eventually cure.

3. Visualize Positive Outcomes

When you train your mind to picture positive possibilities instead of focusing solely on fear or failures, you're conditioning your brain to focus on new possibilities for a new reality.

4. Acknowledge Past Wins as Proof of Future Potential

By reflecting on moments when you overcame past challenges, presents you with strong evidence that you are capable of doing so again. Recognizing past success strengthens self-belief and promotes self-confidence for future challenges.

Anxiety and depression often distorts one's self-perception. Remembering your resilience restores faith in your ability to navigate current and future struggles.

5. Embrace Uncertainty as a Growth Opportunity

Accept that life's uncertainties can lead to new possibilities and personal growth, even when it feels uncomfortable and unfamiliar.

By reframing uncertainty as an opportunity to learn and grow, you greatly reduce fear-driven reactions. Additionally, embracing uncertainty shifts your focus from fear to curiosity, this is another opportunity for progress and healing.

6. Focus on the Present Moment

Have faith that managing the present moment is going to create a better future. Depression often anchors you in the past, while anxiety has you worrying about the future. Focusing on the now builds trust in your ability to be fully present, moment by moment, each and every day.

Believing in what you cannot see involves trusting in the process, visualizing success, learning from past resilience, embracing uncertainty, staying present, and cultivating a hopeful future. When practiced daily, these lessons will build a new paradigm that nurtures healing while reminding you that patience prevails and brighter days are just up ahead.

EXERCISE: How to Build Belief in Unseen Possibilities for Hope, Resilience, and Positive Change.

How it Works:

By setting small, achievable goals and recognizing even minor progress, you reinforce the habit of movement. Focusing on manageable steps makes the path seem less overwhelming.

Why it Works:

The following steps of action help you develop trust in yourself, the process of healing and create a vision for a brighter future.

SIX ACTION STEPS:

#1. "The Seed of Change" Visualization

- Sit quietly and close your eyes.

- Imagine planting seeds in a field of fertile soil. Picture yourself watering and nurturing it daily, although the seeds are unseen.

- Visualize the seeds slowly sprouting into healthy trees over time as a symbol of your healing process.

Just because you aren't seeing immediate results doesn't mean it's not happening.

#2. "Evidence of Resilience" Journal Exercise

Each day become highly aware of any challenges you overcome. Notice the strategy of actions and thoughts that created a support system to help you overcome those challenges. Then spend a few minutes reflecting on how those experiences prove your capacity for growth, even when the outcome wasn't initially clear.

Depression and anxiety often distort self-perception. Applying this action step will acknowledge past wins and begin to teach your brain to trust in your resilience.

3. Daily Affirmations of Trust

Here is an example of affirmations that you can apply today that will quickly begin to reinforce a belief in unseen progress:

- "I am healing, and I trust that small steps will lead to big changes."

- "I am perfectly balanced and complete!"

- " I am a miracle in God's highest form of creation!"

When you make affirmations part of your daily practice, you reprogram the subconscious thought patterns that counters any negative narratives that are often perpetuated by anxiety and depression.

#4. "Uncertainty to Opportunity" Reframing

The next time you experience a situation that feels uncertain or overwhelming, name three potential positive outcomes or opportunities this situation could create.

Opportunities for personal growth build resilience through adversity by reframing your perspective from fear to possibility, helping you cope with uncertainty rather than being carried away by worst-case scenarios.

#5. "Anchor in the Present"

Whenever you consciously focus on your breath, you're also practicing mindfulness. In all of the exercises that included breath work, they always had a profound effect on how quickly I could get my mind to focus on the present moment. The past is gone, the future hasn't arrived, so the only moment we ever truly have is the present moment.

#6. Gratitude for the Unseen

I would strongly encourage you to make gratitude a minute by minute practice until it becomes ingrained in your subconscious as a habit. Below are a few examples of how you can begin the habit of "I AM" gratitude affirmations right now:

- "I AM grateful for the strength I am building, right now!"

- "I AM grateful for the happiness I am creating, right now!"

- "I AM grateful for God's support, right now!"

Daily Reflections (Repeat Daily for the Week)

Write or reflect on these questions each day to strengthen your awareness and shift your mindset in real time.

1. Today I became aware of a thought that didn't serve me. That thought was:

   → Replace it with a more empowering thought:

2. I visualized my future self feeling _____.

   → What did that version of me believe about life, healing, and myself?

3. A small moment of emotional victory I experienced today:

   → (Even a breath, a smile, or a pause counts.)

4. Today I chose to show myself love by:

   → (Action, mindset, or self-care choice.)

5. One word that describes how I want to feel tomorrow:

Weekly Reflection (Complete at the End of the Week)

Use these questions to process the week's progress and recommit to your healing.

1. What limiting belief or emotion did I begin to break free from this week?

2. When did I feel most aligned with the version of me I'm becoming?

3. What inner resistance showed up? How did I respond to it?

4. What insights or wins did I experience this week, no matter how small?

5. What is one powerful intention I'm carrying into next week?

   → My intention:

Optional Weekly Practice

Visualization Activation: Spend 5–10 minutes in meditation or quiet reflection. Imagine your healed, whole, future self. What do you see, feel, and believe? Journal about it.

Anchor Phrase: Choose a simple mantra to repeat each morning this week.

→ Example: "I am free. I am healing. I am enough."

→ Your phrase:

_____

Chapter Eight

Your Breakthrough is Inevitable

Y OU'VE MADE IT TO the final pages of this book, and that means something powerful—you're not the same person who started reading.

You've absorbed new ideas, challenged old beliefs, and opened yourself up to the possibility of a life free from the weight of depression. That alone is a victory.

I want you to take a moment and let this truth sink in: **I believe in you.** I believe in your ability to rewrite your story, to take control of your mind, and to break free from anything that has ever made you feel trapped. Why? Because you're here, right now, proving that you are willing to take a bold step in making emotional freedom your new reality.

You are not broken. You are not powerless. You are not destined to suffer.

You've been given the tools. You know what to do. And now, it's time to step into the next chapter of your life with full confidence.

Think about it—why **wouldn't** you succeed? You've got a plan. You've got the blueprint. And most importantly, **you've got you.** Your mind is the most powerful force you own, and now you're deciding to take charge of it, nothing can stand in your way.

This isn't just wishful thinking. It's reality. You are already transforming, and momentum is on your side. Keep pushing forward. Keep believing. Keep proving to yourself that **depression is NOT your destiny.**

Your new future is waiting for you—stronger, freer, and better than ever. Now go claim it!

Chapter Nine

Helpful Resources

Depression Free: Your Daily Dose of Hope & Strength

A free two-week daily email inspiration to encourage you, support you, and help you stay on track.

https://depressionfreemindset.com/dailydose/

Join Me on YouTube:

https://www.youtube.com/@BFKNBOLD

Let's Stay in Touch:

DepressionFreeMindset.com

Books I Recommend

Becoming Supernatural by Dr. Joe Dispenza

You Are The Placebo by Dr. Joe Dispenza

Breaking the Habit of Being Yourself by Dr. Joe Dispenza

At Your Command by Neville Goddard

Feeling is the Secret by Neville Goddard

Born Rich by Bob Proctor

The Importance of a Solid Support System

Thank you to Lena, and my family for always being there and supporting me through the darkest moments of my life. Your love and care helped me find the strength to keep going.